Alice in
Winterland

Alice in
Winterland
Julie Egdell

STACK
BOOKS

Smokestack Books
1 Lake Terrace, Grewelthorpe, Ripon HG4 3BU
e-mail: info@smokestack-books.co.uk
www.smokestack-books.co.uk

Cover image from the
1981 Soviet animation
Алиса в Стране Чудес.

ISBN 9780995563599

Smokestack Books
is represented
by Inpress Ltd

To my parents,
for their love
and guidance.

Contents

Alisa v Stranye Chudes

I fell down
the rabbit hole.
Now I wear the rabbit
as a coat.

Its skin smells
salty and ancient.
Its fur a gift
for the long winter.

In wonderland
they call me Alisa –
only Alice here is nasty,
not nice.

Black hair,
strong cheekbones,
acid tongued
and scowling.

She is carved
from the permafrost.
Eyes like chipped sapphires.
Выпей меня

on the vodka bottle –
the drink makes you
stronger and healthier,
or shrinks and blinds you,

Note
'Alisa v Stranye Chudes' (Алиса в Стране Чудес) is the Russian for 'Alice in Wonderland'.
'Выпей меня' ('Vuipei minya') means 'drink me' in Russian.

depending on the brand.
In wonderland
cats don't grin
and the caterpillar

is a sick worm
sending tasty smoke rings
dancing in karaoke bars
that never sleep.

Ешь меня.
I eat Soviet donuts
in grandma's kitchen.
Everything tastes

of survival.
What is this world?
Vertical villages
hide soviet

complacency
mixed with Slavic pride.
The tower block reads
Настя я тебя ❤

Nastya ya tibya lyublu
Nastya I love you.
Each floor
a different letter.

How did he do it –
scale the side
of the block
on a rope?

Note
'Ешь меня' ('Yesh minya') . means 'eat me' in Russian.
'Настя я тебя ❤' ('Nastya ya tibya lyublu') means 'Nastya I love you' in
Russian.

And why?
Had Nastya died?
Maybe a fight?
Did Nastya feel the same?

Alongside blocks
monuments to capitalism –
MEGA malls
and McDonald's.

And then, further out,
dachas built by hand
from forest wood
in the war.

Embarrassments
to nouveau Russia's
mansions.
The villages of Piter

a playground
for the rich.
Traffic jams –
Lada's next to Land Rovers.

In wonderland
we feed
birds and squirrels
by hand,

grow our own
in the absence of
currency –
we know

that supermarket stuff
comes from Chernobyl.
We pick mushrooms and berries –
grandma knows which

don't kill you
or send you crazy.
Every year in Spring
police extract

cars and people
from the Neva –
those who went ice fishing
wound up being the catch.

In wonderland
I am a stranger.
I drink tea
from china cups

in tiny apartments
shared by big families,
without choices.
In wonderland

snowflakes
are innocence.
Dust and dirt
homeless and limbless

vanish in the snow.
It washes away the past,
and changing, it rests.
Canals freeze over

the long winter grips.
In wonderland
there's no evil queen,
but years of evil kings.

Deformed foetuses,
pickled in vodka,
line palace walls.
Whispers of

an evil
that never
sleeps.

The Caterpillar Worm

He had always believed
he was a caterpillar
tipped for the top.

But found out
during puberty
he was a worm

with a deformity
of the feet.
Gnarled stumps

on a shattered pelvis.
His arms were simply
disproportionate

to his body –
not destined
to become wings.

To sit on a mushroom cloud
and smoke crack
was surely

a natural reaction
to news like that?
His street end eyes

met me, me them.
What was once
his face.

If I could describe it –
a rotten old orange peel
with two eyes

the colour
of goldfish skin.
Amber, translucent

with all the years in.
Him – a dog
who could take

my arm off.
Someone had
once told him

he had a face
like an egg.
Others said

an arse crack.
Buttons were sewed
into his slimy

worm skin.
Pink, convulsing,
hated.

Covered in the dirt
he couldn't help
living in.

The Caterpillar Worm's Work

I've decided to chronicle
the beautiful demise
of our town,
one track mark
at a time.

The boarded up shops
and bars, the disused factories,
matching my closing down veins,
the shutting up shop
of my immune system,
the protest
of my bowel movements.

I won't stop
until there's
barely an organ working,
barely a bar left serving,
barely a fingernail growing,
barely a hotel open.

This beautiful demise
will be
total.

I'll turn away
all tourists
with a flash
of my hungry eyes and
squawk of my hollow voice
as it asks, without blame,
for spare change.

In the Wood of No Names

I am asked
кто ты?
Who are you?

But can't
remember.
First they call

me Yulia,
then Alisa –
on account

of my being
English
and dark haired.

In this Soviet city
there were no childhoods
watching capitalist Disney.

They tell me
I am just like her.
In the absence

of you,
my imagined
paradise,

there can only be
drowning
of voices.

I have lost hope.
You cut
my hair,

I bought
your clothes.
You sang to me,

I read to you.
You rolled
the joints,

I poured
the drinks.
Usually we said

what we meant.
But sometimes
we didn't.

You went
wherever I led
and I left the

breadcrumbs
of my heart
in all our places

in place of
your passion.
But later

I couldn't find my way back –
you had eaten
them all.

The Real Alisa

Sweet Alisa
all grown up.
Adulthood is
so destroying.

A plastic surgeon
you spend your days
telling patients
it's dangerous

to talk.
Spend your nights eating
99 Kopeck ice cream
with your daughter.

Dreaming of a land
where husbands
could be
at home.

You remember
childhood summers
at your grandfather's dacha
in the Ukraine.

Collecting warm
eggs at dawn,
the bitterness of
berries

ripe from the sun.
One day he dies,
suddenly,
and you, at 33,

notice
childhood
is gone.
You cried

that day.
Learning English
because you too
believe there is

a better life,
a better place.
You fall in love
with me –

the English Alice
of your childhood.
Because you still believe
in wonderland.

Disney Alice

A young scientist
who works in a café
decides upon a theme –
Alice in Wonderland.

She has long, blonde hair
emerald eyes which hurt
what they touch.
A hidden smile.

She thinks I am Alice.
She falls in love with me
and England, but gets
to know us better.

She borrows a white rabbit.
Dresses as the Disney Alice,
the inventor of a dreamland
in a Petergof cafe,

but is disappointed –
Petergof's MEGA mall
shoppers don't know
Disney Alice.

Where is your dark hair?
Your sarcastic smile?
Your sharp fringe?
Your white dress?

Young Baba Yaga

I can scarcely believe what has happened to me.
Betrayed by my love, chased from the town.
Now I live alone in the forest and catch spiders
in the unearthly twilight.
Sometimes I am a spider too,
hiding in a web of my own making.

I hallucinate strange monsters.
I don't know if they are real or if I have made them.
I know my mother had these visions too.
She told me to control it.
It is said that all the trouble
came from my great grandmother.

There is no magic or beauty left in me.
This incessant light makes me look old.
I have to find a way to get the old light back.
I am bitter with longing.
Remembering, with pain, the warmth of his lips
the feeling of him deep within,

how it opened my whole being
how it felt this was the only thing on earth I was made for.
Every memory is a small death.
I grow turnips, keep chickens,
surrounded by silence.
Animals, at least, are not afraid of me.

Note:
Baba Yaga is a witch in Slavic folk-tales. She flies through the forest in a
mortar and pestle and lives in a house that stands on chicken legs.

Tongue

My tongue licks my teeth
when I lisp my way around
languages.

It flicks, air blowing, it
gently makes that
hissssss.

My tongue is kissed
accent, dialect
words,

which fit in the
landscape of
childhood.

Outside this
it loses its colour,
it's intensity.

I search for an answer
to the question of
my Russia.

Sounding out the
'kchuh'
[x]

and the
'uiy'
[ы].

Note:
The Russian letters 'x' (kchuh) and 'ы' (uiy) are hard for non-Russian
speakers to pronounce.

I listen and repeat,
follow strangers
in the street,

curl my tongue,
fall in love
with words.

And I write,
write,
ПИСАТЬ!

In curly,
whirly,
cursive.

And I read,
read,
ЧИТАТЬ!

Underlining
what I don't
understand.

And I eat,
eat,
ЕСТЬ!

Borsch,
blini
and black bread.

Note
The russian words 'писать' ('pisat'), 'читать' ('chitat') and 'есть' ('yest') are
the verbs to write, read and eat.

And I drink,
drink
ПИТЬ!

Wine and
water and
beer.

And I speak,
speak,
ГОВОРИТЬ!

As an experiment
I begin at the beginning.

Note
The Russian words 'пить' ('pit') and 'говорить' ('gavarit') are the verbs to drink and speak.

Alice in Wonderland Syndrome

She told me her body was always changing.
Bits of it were too big,
others too small.

It didn't matter
what diet
she was on.

It was something
to do with
the bones,

the tendons,
the ligaments.
She said she bound bits

of herself up
when people
weren't looking.

Trying to stop
the swelling,
the bulging.

Monstrous
disfigurations –
the curvature

of the spine,
the hunchback
that was there

one day,
gone the next.
She even slept

for a time
in a homemade coffin!
To allow

no surprise
growths
overnight.

But this
didn't stop
the shrinking

and once
she woke
to find

one leg
the size
of a Barbie (she said).

And the
other one
swinging

very close
to her eyes.
The changes

to herself,
to the world
intangible.

What's worse, she said,
was that movement
was not only futile

but near impossible.
That she spent her days
running on a

conveyor belt
going
nowhere.

Baba Yaga Bags a Man

They sent him to take me,
in the end I took him.
I swear I didn't try anything,
but magic is the blood in my veins.

He brought a cage to take
me to my trial. We spent three days
in bed, he couldn't get enough.
I liked his eyes best, and his smile.

That intense way he would just
stare at me, like he couldn't help
himself (which, of course, he couldn't).
He loved my cooking too.

It was great – to have someone
around to chop the wood.
But in the end his wife came
and brought their son.

I'm not a monster,
I'd had my fun,
so I let him go
and he left me a gift –

a daughter
arrived in Spring.

White Stone Days

A great deal has been misunderstood.
So try to understand.

I am Dodgson,
not Carroll –

shy, stammering,
abused, abusing.

There were two choices –
the church or the army.

I chose neither.
I was born to a father

disappointed
with life

a mother
who lived hers for us –

me and ten siblings,
hundreds of cousins.

I liked noise,
liked family.

Sometimes we had money
most times we didn't.

The rectory umbrella
couldn't contain us.

I repress three years
in boarding schools –

daytime fights,
night-time disturbances

I wouldn't repeat.
I try to forget

with London and lights,
too many female friends.

It's true I was cursed –
I had a stammer

which is indicative
of nothing

other than
I had a stammer.

I liked singing,
by the way.

The theatre,
storytelling,

photography.
Beauty was divinity,

smiles could save.
Aestheticism

and morality
go hand in hand.

I went to Oxford
because it was

the next bit of the plan
but had to return

after two days –
my mother had died.

I grieved the loss
to my life.

It took my
whole life and more

to understand
how much.

After studying
I lectured in Maths.

I hated it,
dreamed of

being a writer.
I'd have liked

nothing better
than not having to work.

Or so I thought, at the time.
All of it seems irrelevant now.

The Liddell's –
that famous friendship.

Poor Alice
they have made two

where there was only one!
Now you and I

are strangers
to our true selves.

The umbrella
was no protection.

It gets everyone
in the end.

All that's left is
memories,

days of white stone.
A tale I took

that wasn't mine
to tell.

The truth is
I was used

to a lot of children.
I liked children,

amongst other things.
I rejected religion

lost the respect
of my father

but was allowed
to remain at Oxford.

Alice was published,
my first success.

I toured Russia –
my only view

of a real Wonderland.
How could I have known,

fresh faced at 19,
Oxford would be

the rest of my life?
My father's death

clouded me.
I could never be

what he wanted.
And finally

I had the money
to leave teaching.

Bought a house
where I lived with

my spinster sisters.
A carousel of bright

nieces and nephews
came and went.

Cheered the place up.
I led a life of leisure

and madness
largely unnoticed.

Then I died
and my myth was born.

The Original Alice

I remember no shoes,
a torn dress,
the river,
an English summer.

Before school
before corsets
before anything.

One hand out,
for forgiveness
one on my hip,
for defiance.

I was an ugly child
everyone agreed –
except him.

Tom boy,
mother called me.
My sisters
couldn't understand
how a little girl
be so vulgar.

His Alice
became a hit
little to do with my life –
his fantasy.

As a young woman,
still one hand for
forgiveness,
one for pride.

There was a hardness in me.
My innocent, wistful look
a twisted glare.
The flowers
in my flowing hair.

I travelled Europe
but was not free.
Memories, like blackbirds,
followed me everywhere.
The corset pinched
strangling me
slowly.

Four great losses:
two sons in the war,
my husband
and finally
my myth.

Sold to pay for the house.
To be free of it
was to be free
of everything
that had mattered.

Now old, fat, balding, alone
there's no-one to ask
for forgiveness anymore.

I sit with hands in lap,
sipping endless tea,
trying to ignore death.
Waiting
for
a final
adventure.

The Road to Vyborg

The road to Vyborg.
I count the dead on my hands,
but run out of fingers.
The road is dangerous

and *this is Russia*,
you say.
You took me from the smoke
to the white castle

where dogs,
half wolf,
greet me like an old friend
and the cave hides Sadko

turned to stone with age.
At your Dacha there is a bear
wrestled and killed
in Murmansk.

And nothing is a mystery.
We drink tea and eat biscuits
like everything is normal.

Note
Sadko is a merchant, adventurer and musician in a medieval Russian epic
poem; also the subject of an opera by Rimsky-Korsakov.

Yelagin Island

First visited in autumn, alone.
No-one wanted to journey
outside the city
that day.

I wanted to see trees
after a long absence.
Shades of autumn,
the Baltic Sea.

The only others were
fisherman, dog walkers.
A dog approached
unhindered by language.

We had an easy exchange.
I went to the end of the island
to see the water which
separates me from my family.

A clear day,
I try to spot my parents
on Tynemouth beach
a thousand miles away.

Later –
when he came to visit
I took him there,
ice skating.

The whole island
transformed by snow
frozen in Leningrad
and still no-one.

There are bears,
reindeer, dancers,
two lovers,
surrounded by flowers
long since dead.
A frozen embrace
outside
white
palace
walls.

Dacha

I locked you in for the winter.
Still not understanding
what is not love.

The icicles were spears.
I punched them
down

a random act
of violence.
We ate and drank

like eating and drinking
could fill us
or make up

for what
you won't
or can't

say.
I don't want you
to leave, I said

over
and
over

like a spell
I could make
come true.

Let's Pretend We're King and Queen

Let's pretend we're King and Queen,
the world a game of chess.
Let's pretend you still love me,
I like it that way best.

Let's pretend I didn't ask you
not to leave, to stay.
And let's pretend you didn't
walk out on me that day.

Let's pretend we're king and queen
not helpless, tiny pawns.
Let's pretend we mean something
at least until the dawn.

Baba's House

She lived in a
jenga house, my baba.
Huge arms of oak
piled gently on top of us.

I tried to count
the age of the house
in coffee coloured rings,
but lost count.

The house was
infested with door demons,
floor creatures,
wolves and gods.

Twisted maroon
slash grin,
amber ochre eye,
or eyes.

Seas of noir waves
separated strands
of golden hair
and deserts

threatened
to steal me away.
A violet shadow,
ancient purple bruise

lived under my bed
behind black bars,
painted by my baba,
to help me sleep.

Alice Meets Alisa in Krash

She hadn't been here for years.
Typical that they would meet now
when she was feeling crumpled
from comments about

pounds collected and dark
circles around the eyes.
*You can't be a little
girl forever.*

She'd heard a lot about this Alisa –
this Russian version of herself.
Heard she was a bitch, fuckin' hard.
Because she was afraid

she had offered a drink,
vodka and soda –
what a cliché.
She was just as people said –

the black hair, the scowl,
even the cheap vodka
didn't cause a shiver.
She was dressed

like a stripper –
dark blue bodycon,
everything on show.
Where is her fear?

Something was muttered
about her sizeable arse,
so she stuck her tongue
between her fingers.

Dark red lipstick left a stain.
Men didn't seem to mind
the arse, preferring to look
at tits, circling around

her ample frame like
sailors to a siren.
The first guy to try his luck
received no reply –

only the obscene
hand gesture
which told him
he was a wanker.

Alisa meets Alice in Krash

So meek, so mild.
English ideas
of politeness
so restrictive.

Why do you laugh
at what is not funny?
Why do you smile
when you are unhappy?

How many STD's Alice got
because she doesn't
understand the word no?
How many times

will she look
from the glass
to the door
to the floor

like someone
will try to eat her whole,
at any moment?
A snack sized treat.

Perfect nightmare
in a blue dress.
More little girl
than woman.

I want to crack her
about the face.
Tell her feminism
Happened

while England was sleeping!

She is a knot of magazine images
and billboards –
the perfect blonde
Disney Alice, as you want.

I know she takes laxatives
like after dinner mints,
spends weeks
eating only fruit,

won't show her legs
unless it's to spread them
can't hold a drink
without spilling it,

can't see a man
without ruining him.
A beautiful bringer
of chaos. She destroys

everything on her own:
the one thing she doesn't
need any help with.

Under the Umbrella

People say –
mothers are more important than milk.

But how would I know?
I've never had one.
I was made and remade
by a man with a pencil.

Dreamchild with no brothers
or sisters. No other children
to play with. I am
my father's experiment.

He makes my life
full of terror and
dark appetite.
I live in a world

where my size
is always changing,
my name always
being forgotten.

My whole world
is his umbrella.
How awful the real
world must be!

Alice Hargreaves

You have no idea
what it's like
to be his creation.

Not just his Alice
but to feel that
all your words

have already
been said.
My life

a script
he wrote.
He said

I haunted him!
But hauntings
work two ways.

I am forever young.
Ghost who can't depart.
Girl who stopped
at seven.

In the Land of Mirrors

In the Land of Mirrors
dreams become nightmares.

It's unclear
if you're asleep
or awake.

My life
is on ice.

Spend my
weekends
pacing the frozen

Neva looking
for Sadko
in the cracks.

I found an Alice
made of pink
and permafrost

frozen dead.

Things get
confused here
we are not quite

ourselves.
After the karaoke bar
I tried to show you

this strip bar –
DJ's shout
ДАВАЙ! there

over house music.
I thought I could
make you enjoy it.

But every corner
only led
to the last.

Empty bottles,
rejected bodies,
littered the cigarette kiosk.

We
who
slide over
black ice
4am
on
dirty
Dumbskaya
street.

Note
'Давай!' (davai!) is the informal imperative of the Russian verb to give. Here the DJs mean something like 'let's go!'

Lessons from the Baba Yaga

Everything is light form.
what I want,
I get.

It arrives to me
as I wished.
You see

magic exists.
I am powerful,
as are you.

You can do
whatever you want.
First comes thought

then reward.
There is no law
of physics.

People,
like everything,
are a series

of shapes
and are nothing
to be afraid of.

If you want them
they are yours.
There is just

taking.
And the taking
is so easy.

Mad Hatter's Tea Party

The Mad Hatter admired her approach
with the violence of the unwell.
Here because there's nowhere else to go.
But what's better than a party

that never ends?
His nose a door handle.
His eyes the screws.
His fingers are all double jointed,

stick out at obtuse angles.
He tended to fall out
with people and scare them off.
He offered her the samogon –

vodka made in his bathtub
in a half-hearted attempt
at an orgy.
She accepted the toast

за любовь
He didn't want to start
anything
and didn't always

enjoy sex
but this girl was different.
He could imagine –
nice shirt, pair of brogues.

Note
Samogon (самогон) is a Russian home-distilled spirit.
The Russian toast за любовь ('za lyubov') is to 'love'

And she in turn could see
a flash of auburn brilliance
in the eyes. Mad and a liar,
but aren't all the best ones?

Aren't all the survivors?
And wasn't she, after all?
The march hare, broken
from gambling

their only drinking
companion.
Substitute for a dad
and they the children.

But this dad comes with skunk
and tonight they roll
and watch clouds pass by
too quickly and worry

sincerely about the
bottom of the galaxy.
Hatter objects to the word mate
but Hare says

She loves mate-ing
Hatter wears earrings
and swaps clothes with Alice.
He is held together

by bolts, pins, needles,
vanity, nails, belts, scarves,
a strong sense of self
and sexual charisma.

I'm what you'll find
when you're not looking
she told him.

I'm everything
you've never wanted.
He tried a witty comeback –
I'm what people do when they don't.
he said, but this was needlessly vague

he had no idea what he'd meant.
The march hare hasn't eaten
for days and is waiting
for results – irritable bowels

or the big C.
He wants to join the game
but he's no contender.
You should say what

you mean he said, angrily.
I do, said Alice
at least I mean what I say.

Is it right to dress your pets
in smoking jackets?
Hatter asked, she didn't answer –
dozing from the drink.

Samogon tended to
silence people.
But he'd never had
any complaints.

I am poisoned, he said
and poison has to come out.
The Hare caught his eye
and silently they did

what needed to be done.
They both hate and need
each other.
It was over
as all they knew at the start

it would be.
As she stumbled away,
Hatter called after:

You should really say what you mean!
'I like what I get' isn't the same as
'I get what I like'!

How the Caterpillar Worm Sees

He doesn't see bright colours.
There's something wrong
with his irises.

They were made
for a life underground.
Most of his days

are unrelentingly grey,
everything in the world
consists of blocks,

not particles.
Things need to be
pared down,

simple.
Black on white,
purple on black.

Lines get blurred –
purple can be tainted
with black –

but nothing
can be changed.
The world is an ocean –

he a piece of plankton,
floating
without sound.

The shadows
on the walls
are of
ladies,
pitchforks,
bulls,
guns,
birds,
dancers,
towers,
fighters,
angels,

a magical
merry go round.

He is not sure
what makes them
project so obscurely there.

Hundreds of them.
Bodies encased in titanium
or made from steel.

When he tries
to see faces
there is nothing.

The creases
of their spines
a mirage.

Alice appears to him,
not form but colour.
A black felt head

with zips for eyes,
a reel of red photo
negatives around her neck.

Alice Meets the Caterpillar Worm

August
rough sleep
dreaming.

Bullet proof police
hold back
barefoot

brides from the brink.
I love the city
like never before –

a fear of death
the key to all joy.
I told him

I was cold and hungry.
He said to try it.
The night is not black

but purple.
The streetlight
on our backs

the floor.
Mobile phones
light up passers by

like Christmas.
They say
the best comedy

is tragedy.
I enjoy being a me
not a 'we'.

I walked the whole town
hypnotised, possessed.
Tried three times

for a fight, but failed.
Carried a knife
since I was 15.

A gift
from a teenage brother
who knows
what boys
are like.

Alice's Evidence

Lawyers forever talk of
child abuse, the care system,
heavy handed sentences
and the lack of rehab centres.

How young you are
but don't look –
as if you're not in
the room.

You're supposed to say
you didn't deserve any of it,
you're supposed to say
not guilty,

but you're not sure
it's true. You see –
one pill makes you bigger,
and one pill makes you small,

until you almost drown
in tears, and sell anything
to anyone
at all.

Lawyers
are forever
shaking, waking you
from sleep.

As you walk
you feel you
tip the room,
disturb the air.

Start at the
start, go on
until the end
then stop,

he says.
You are not yourself –
can't remember things
like you used to.

You remember only
being burned out,
being turfed out,
being cleaned out.

Rock runs,
rock houses,
then halfway houses
with strict drug rules.

Wanting to burn
fast and high
in flames of silver,
that flicker out.

Something from Alice

I couldn't have stayed in dread filled childhood.
Even in the homemade pink chiffon princess dress
with the crown that glittered and won the prize
smashing the blossom petals off the tree
so everyone could see –
today was my wedding day.

I disappeared from the garden shed one afternoon.
Floated bloated and pale down an English stream,
my skin expanding and hardening,
to emerge the taller version of everyone's little sister.
Alone now – except for the creatures.
Rodents assembled from clock parts,

red stain dolls clothes, bright brass buttons,
fixed dead marble eyes, assorted animal teeth
set into stuffed carcasses that may or may not
have been alive, once.
Tormented and chased
where there is no hiding place.

One day I found the shed, ran in and locked the door.
My skin had grown harder now, a thick marble prison.
I fell back from the weight of myself,
surrendered to black insides
feeling weightless and tired now.
I emerged from the belly of my outer skin.

What I had been lay below me,
her belly split open, skin frozen porcelain,
varnished eyes still moving, still blinking.
Years ago her mouth had dried up with the rest of me,
unable to speak, she blinked diamond tears away.
I took my father's hammer and smashed her

into tiny white pieces which melted
like snowflakes. I opened the shed door
one last time to the garden of my childhood.
Only the stump remained of where the blossom
tree had been. A clothes prop in its place.
White linens floating in an afternoon chill.

This was not childhood anymore.

Dreamchild

'Come, hearken then, ere voice of dread,
With bitter tidings laden,
Shall summon to unwelcome bed
A melancholy maiden!
We are but older children, dear,
Who fret to find our bedtime near.'

Lewis Carroll, *Through the Looking Glass*

Last night
I played the nothing game
again.

It's like being born –
in reverse,
they say.

It's like un-singing
yourself a lullaby.
Breathing away

every word
one by one
into the dark.

Shushing yourself
into numbness.
We know

so much,
understand
so little.

Imagine –
if death was just
a matter of not living.

If everything
that was real was unchanging,
unchangeable.

If going to sleep
was just a matter
of closing my eyes.

You told me life is brief
and there is something
to be feared,

but you never said what.
Life
is all consuming

– it will
get us
all.

Some people say
that death
is forever
but
I
can't
believe
that.

Sometimes I think I am dead,
but physical pain
stands me corrected.

Some people say that everything
is connected
by a universal law.

Day and night.
Hot and cold.
Constantly in flux.

The world
a state
of ever change –

that you can never
step into
the same river
twice.

Some people say
that's bullshit.
That which exists
cannot also not exist

so that the void
is impossible
change
is impossible.

Everything
that is
always was
and always
will be.

People smile
talk of far away eyes,
forgetfulness,

how I
always go
for the bad ones.

They talk about
bar fights,
twisted ankles, poison

like it's rock and roll
the actions
of a bitch –

in a Hollywood
kind of way.
They talk about

Disney Tuesdays,
lucky dip Wednesdays
and half litre Thursdays

like these are
the days
of our lives.

I tell myself
there is a life
not like this.

Play the nothing game,
again
but always
lose.

Ask Alice

What makes a person
seek out rabbit holes?

All of my friends
are mad in many ways.

Some escaping –
poverty, religion, cancer.

Some trying
to get somewhere.

All of us are visitors
in wonderland –

museum of dreams,
disappointments,

lost childhood.
We spend weekends

in forever open
Dumbskaya bars –

smoke shisha, drink vodka,
bum cigarettes in

broken Russian.
We spend most of our time

walking on thin ice.
Make friends

in leather jackets.
Drink beer by the canals,

eat sharma in
24 hour places.

We leave each other
for dead.

With hangovers
we walk round and round

the town, wondering.
We watch fireworks

and thunderstorms.
We collect leaves in autumn

drink honey beer in winter
climb on rooftops.

We are always eating
or drinking something.

Twisted picnics
of deadly liquors

England's roasts,
America's Thanksgiving.

Our appetites are scary
but we can't seem to stop.

We stay awake in white nights
wandering the streets

wave our flags at the parade
with all the rest

like we belong.
We bitch about

UK, USA and yes,
sometimes USSR.

But mostly
Russia is a mother

who accepts

our sadness gladly,
our darkness knowingly,

our failings happily –
no questions asked.

The Ice Road, the Bone City, the Blood Church

I live in the Bone city
the serfs built.
Their bones sealed
into the foundations.
The city
their graveyard.
The city's population
their mourners.
What was rock
becomes rock again.

Inside my Bone city
the Blood church.
Built on spilled blood,
saved by spilled blood.
And the blood
that the city was spilled on
and the blood
that was spilled on the city,
is worshipped here
by the faithful –

who know
as long as blood
can be spilled,
it will be spilled
again and again.

The Ice road,
a gallery of
toddler bones.
Flung from their mothers arms
by drivers desperate
to leave the burning city
deaf to pleas
to stop, or turn back.
Bone and ice,
city and blood,

what was rock
will become rock.
And I listen
to the stories
that the dead
have to tell.
On my Ice road,
in my Blood church,
in my Bone city.

Alice in USA Land

The rectory umbrella
could never hold us.
You wrote me a life
I could never have

in a land
I would never know.
Born into a family name
my marriage bed

decided by a bank balance.
How dare you make me feel
there was a choice,
that I was free,

that love was
for the ruling class.
I am a girl – not a
piece in a puzzle.

The only thing we had
under the umbrella
were lies, secrets, heartache
at a safe distance.

Myths of our own making.
At age 80 I have been invited
to America to tell the lies
we started all those years ago.

I showed you with one look
all you had meant to me.
But I am grateful to you
for my myth, it's made me

immortal, and more important
than I am. I'd give all that up
for a life unknown
where I could have loved

and been loved.
My love dead
two sons dead
my husband dead

and you, Mr Dodgson.
A man whose name
was even a mystery.
In my old age

I am left with myself
in every edition
in every language
a thousand versions

of that famous
summer day.
The clouds that became sun,
a tale we all tell so well.

I collect them all
never forgetting
those days
in wonderland.

The tale more powerful
than the memory.
In wonderland you had me
take control

become queen.
Now I sit on graves –
dreamchild
for whom fear,

death and terror
are lessons to be learned
over more than a lifetime.
I listen to the gulls,

the trees and try
to forget September.
Count blessings,
get done wondering.

A roof over my head
more important than myths,
in the end.

In and Out the Rabbit Hole

I've slipped back
to my old life
like putting on
last winter's glove.

So easy,
yet impossible to go back.
I am sitting with candles.
And everything

is as simple
and as difficult
as I want it to be.
It is quiet

and the knowledge
I could be here
where I've been
so many times before

will haunt me
in every lonely moment.
When the moon
comes out,

an old friend,
it is the same moon
I prayed to in India.
I've dismantled a life

and started a new lie.
This room.
I left in such a hurry
never looked back.

All the things
I left behind.
Little comforts
forgotten.

This vast window,
this night,
this moon,
this silence.

The Baba Yaga's Secret

She digs up the fruit of her labour
the size of a child's heart, almost beating.
She slices off the skin of each orb.
The thick red trickles down her hands.
She licks the bitter bleeding
from her rheumatic fingers.

It's the beets that have
made her live this long –
not magic. Magic can't do that.
She cooks borsch every day.
Blood red stains keep people
off her land, saved her from

witch trials – she was feared enough.
Every village needs a villain.
Sometimes desperation conquers fear.
People come and ask for a healing
or ask her what really happened
to their sons and daughters.

Alisa v Zazerkale

The longest winter.
Life stagnates –
stands still
with the freezing

of the Neva.
I long for –
home? You?
Or is it

the familiar?
Without fear
or mystery,
with too much time,

I spend my days
in silent wonder.
Lost in songs
and chemical dreams.

Trying to escape
the truth –
I am alone.
Do you remember

that lonely child?
Aren't you still her?
The definition of madness –
I spent a whole day

Note
"Alisa v Zazerkale' (Алиса в Зазеркалье) is the Russian for 'Alice Through the Looking Glass'.

hungover, watching films
on a tiny screen
while people led lives
outside.

Exiled from my language
exiled from my life.
The lesser the challenge
the worse the living

it seems.
In the suburbs
reverence and awe
surrounds me.

The loneliness of
not understanding,
the emptiness
of not belonging.

I am the land –
jokes and Tories
gin in teacups
red and black and white

land of August riots
land of five bags
land of fit to work
land of benefit cuts.

They look at me and see
The Queen, red telephone boxes
Sherlock Holmes, Harry Potter

The Tower of London
Madame Tussauds
and me – falling down
a rabbit hole,

helping myself to
another cake
at the Mad Hatter's
tea party.

Refugee, escaping
an evil queen
who wants the head's
of the poor.

They call me Alisa
they wonder where
my teapot is (we always
use them, don't we?)

I am from a land,
they say,
whose clocks have stopped
at five.

I am from the land,
they say,
where it's always
time for tea.

The Last 24 hours in Wonderland

The moon is out again
saying goodbye.
The days grow shorter
and colder.

It seems an age
since a summer of possibilities
spread-out
before me.

Soon it will be time
to step, blinking,
out of Wonderland.
Away from life

as it could be
if time stopped.
But life,
I tell myself,

is worth living.
Tomorrow
my last 24 hours
in Wonderland.

What is Wonderland?
An absorption of the mind
and the senses.
A physical

and intellectual pleasure.
An unawareness
of the passing
of time.

A living
death.

Notes

The Caterpillar Worm
'What was once his face' is a reference to Anna Akhmatova queuing outside prison to see her son during the Stalin purges in Petersburg:

"One day somebody in the crowd identified me. Standing behind me was a woman, with lips blue from cold, who had, of course, never heard me called by name before. Now she started out of the torpor common to us all and asked me in a whisper (everyone whispered there): 'Can you describe this?'

And I said: 'I can.'

Then something like a smile passed fleetingly over what had once been her face."
(Anna Akhmatova, *Requiem*, 1963)

Alice Meets Alisa in Krash
Krash was the name of a now defunct bar in Newcastle.

The Mad Hatter's Tea Party
Some of the lines in this poem come from the chapter of the same name in *Alice in Wonderland*.

Alice's Evidence
The title as well as some of the lines of this poem come from the chapter of the same name in *Alice in Wonderland*. 'One pill makes you bigger and one pill makes you small' refers to the Jefferson Airplane song 'White Rabbit'.

Something from Alice
This poems is a response to the Czech animation *Neco z Alenky* (Something from Alice) directed by Jan Svankmajer.

Alisa v Zazerkale
'Gin in teacups' is from the Babyshambles song 'Albion'.

Acknowledgements

Thanks goes to Andy Willoughby – a true sensei – for over ten years of support and friendship. Thanks to to Bob Beagrie, a great teacher, to Rowan McCabe for helping to edit the collection and to P.A. Morbid for encouragement and advice when it was needed.

Thanks are also due to the editors of the following publications where some of these poems were first published: *Black Light Engine Room, French Literary Review, Ink Sweat and Tears, Streetcake, Dark Matter 4*; also Bob Beagrie and Andy Willoughby (eds) *The Breakout Anthology* (2013).